MW01037397

KINGDOM

Books by Joesph Millar

Overtime
Fortune
Ocean
Blue Rust
Kingdom

Chapbooks

Slow Dancer
Nightbound
Bestiary
Duet (with Dorianne Laux)

KINGDOM

Joseph Millar

Carnegie Mellon University Press
Pittsburgh 2017

Acknowledgments

Thank you to the editors of these magazines, where some of these poems first appeared:

Academy of American Poets, Poem-a-Day: "One Day"
American Poetry Review: "Southern Exposure," "Ancestral," "Community Hospital," "Eclipse," "Mothers"
Blackbird: "Black Pan"
The Boiler Journal: "The Poem of Experience"
Brilliant Corners: "Monk"
Catamaran: "Lovesick"
Chicago Quarterly Review: "Calling Home," "Oxygen and Acetylene"
december: "End of the World"
Great River Review: "Semi-Retired"
Labor: "Paris Rain"
Mead: "Artist Colony"
Miramar: "Night"
New Letters: "The Day After Sinatra," "Valentine"
The North (UK): "Why Women Live Longer"
Ploughshares: "The Poetry-Body," "Girlfriends"
Plume: "Muse," "Field"
Poetry Bay: "Ronnie: 1954 – 2013"
Prairie Schooner: "Making Lunch," "Patience," "Courtly," "For Ruth Stone," "Bad Love Affair"
River Styx: "Clair de Lune"
San Pedro River Review: "Reckoning"
The Swamp: "Torch Singer"
Terminus: "Roses"
Tin House: "Right Livelihood," "Night Light"
Willow Springs: "Next to Godliness"

Many thanks to the generosity of the Guggenheim Foundation and to the Virginia Center for the Creative Arts. Thanks to Pacific University's MFA. Thanks also to Marvin Bell, Tim McBride, David St. John, Stephen Dobyns, Kwame Dawes, Shelley Washburn, and Chuck Millar. Thanks especially to John-Roger, John Morton and Dorianne Laux.

Cover art: David Garratt, *Furn Coe*, 2013. Collage, 69" x 109". Photo by Paige Critcher.

Book design by Connie Amoroso

Library of Congress Control Number 2016948991
ISBN 978-0-88748-621-0
Copyright © 2017 by Joseph Millar
All rights reserved
Printed and bound in the United States of America

10 9 8 7 6 5 4 3 2

for Peter Everwine

Contents

"The sun is new again, every day."

—Heraclitus

The Poem of Experience

"I will never again write from personal experience."
                                        —Jean-Paul Darien

If they keep on with their incessant muttering,
chipping away at the worn first person
now pulling weeds in the garden
or leaning its ladder against the garage,
maybe no one else will show up
in sneakers and old musty hat
to water the lettuce or clean out the gutters,
patch up the broken gate. . . .

Maybe no one will waste most of Wednesday
driving to town and getting lost
on the slanted black streets of Lynchburg
amid coffee galleries and book stores, the music
CDs glittering like badges: Hendrix, Mingus,
the jewelry of cell phones opening
their cheap clasps over the sidewalks
dotted with late spring rain.

Maybe the kitchen above the brick steps
will vanish in a sudden postmodern ellipsis,
along with the olive oil in its jar
glowing like a lamp on the counter top
strewn with the gold skin of carrots and spuds
and the onion's translucent husks,
the pot with a glass lid
bought at Good Will,
the stove's charred burner
and blue gas flame even now
beginning to stutter and rise,
even now beginning to hiss.

Time-Poem

No one will tell me
where the horses have gone
who rested under the oak trees
especially the black one with mottled lips
who would hum to himself
when I stroked his chest fur
nicked up by barbwire and covered
with flies, beneath which his huge
and sleepless heart
carried him into the summer,
his ghost now grazing the roadside
this night before the Florida Derby.

The pasture's a canebrake of ancient kudzu
laid down and braided with rusted fence,
the road a wide strip of moonlit ashes
leading away from the barn
where my friend makes his sculptures
of clay and branched iron,
unchanged by time

though Jupiter hangs low overhead,
like us unable to escape the hours.
It's two in the morning on the coast
of the moon, but here it's just midnight
and the sleepers open their arms
to the sound of 5,000 horses
driving the big train south from Monroe,
dragging the long cars mile after mile,
its engineer like an aging king
watching the clock, one hand on the throttle,
the howl of the whistle under the stars,
trapped and burning.

Right Livelihood

The little stream runs all the way down
under the long cracked sills
of the parking lot
mostly abandoned now,
shadows gathering
in the busted marquee
of the discount tobacco store
with its wire hangers
and dusty stairs,
its candles stuck
in their squat mason jars
vanilla and sandalwood, blueberry, pine—
whose proprietor doesn't carry your brand
and keeps chattering into a cell phone
a dialect of some distant land
under the brim of his hat.
Thence to the glass doors
of Anna's Linens
Going Out of Business Sale
where you buy four pillows and a bathmat
for 35 bucks
then sit shotgun, one foot on the floor
the other smudging the dash
eating Taco Bell and describing
your ideal poet's job in this life.
More of a career than a job really,
more of a calling than a career:
to own and manage a combination
lavender-farm-bed-and-breakfast
which would smell great, of course
and glow faintly purple
and feature tall windows,

a balcony in each room
where smoking would be permitted—
which would also specialize in prostitution
for a clientele in late middle age
whose demands might no longer
be strenuous
or even particularly lewd—
maybe they would mostly desire
to be gently chided
in a husky voice
or even spoken to kindly,
their toes washed in rosewater,
their foreheads soothed
in the breeze from a porch swing,
then wrapped in Egyptian cotton
and fed Belgian chocolate
blindfolded.

We gas up and head west
into the mountains of Carolina
worn down by time
by snow and heat,
new pillows piled up in the back seat.

Muse

Who can tell how she got here
in her headdress and midnight braids,
drifting ashore in a black skiff
and planting the seeds of 2012
she stole from the early Mayans
next to the golf course pond
where the young boys in Phoenix
go fishing at night for the shadowy cats
that lie just off the bottom
in their spiky whiskers and rayed fins.
When they hook a big one, they snap
a quick trophy-photo
keeping an eye out for the watchman.

No one can tell when she'll be back
carrying her cup of embalming fluid
and her book about primitive shame
though we wait for her in the paisley chair,
entering each evening quietly
with someone sick in the other bed
of a gray motel where she might
be found, random police sirens
strobing the neighborhood.

But she is not thinking of beauty or death
only the wet shoes and denim,
the beer cans collected and desert stars
shining like salvaged metal
and the big fish released
sinking back to the bottom
to feed on the muddy stems—
its strange flat head and narrow lips,
its naked, electric-blue skin.

Semi-Retired

Sometimes the most I do all day
is wander the grocery aisles in a trance
looking for a deal on yellow onions
or a half-pound of lunch meat.
Back home I watch
the city's backhoe
digging a trench in the street.
This is the life, I say to myself,
whiff of coffee and cotto salami,
whiff of broken-up asphalt.

At seventy I keep waking up
next to my father's corpse,
supine in necktie and herringbone vest,
blue shirt spattered with wine.
Get out of my way, I tell him,
watching the nurse arrive
sent by the new insurance company
to measure my vitals and blood.

I try to keep quiet during the week
though I love my small-time anonymous self
breaking jars in the trash bin
destructive and silent and grandiose,
lost in its dreams of ashes and theft
and speaking about them to no one.

And my body seems like a sister,
sister of fluids and oxygen,
sister of sleep in the afternoon.
I roll up my sleeve and hold out
my arm to the home nurse resting

her thumb on my wrist,
looking down at her watch
like an overweight angel of mercy
listening to the blood
running back to the heart,
telling me to breathe and let go.

One Day

Everything shimmers
with the sound of the train
rattling over the bridge,
especially the ears and nostrils and teeth
of the horse riding out
to the pasture of breath
where the long freight runs
on diesel fuel
that used to run on coal.
I keep listening
for the crickets and birds
and my words fall down below.

I mistook the train for a thunderstorm,
I mistook the willow tree
for a home, it's nothing to brag about
when you think of it,
spending this time all alone.
I wandered into the hayfield
and two ticks jumped in my hair.
They dug in my scalp
and drank up my blood
like the sweet wine of Virginia,
then left me under the Druid moon
down here on earth in the kingdom.

Next to Godliness

I like to sit with the door wide open
listening to March rain gush down my street,
wearing a blue hat from the Outer Banks
and pondering the cleanliness of porn stars,
John Holmes and Traci Lords,
their pale bodies hairless as sea creatures
glistening with K-Y or Astro-Glide
under the tender lights.

Sometimes the storm drains
jam up with leaves
and the blond neighbor
who lives by herself
and is too old to be a porn star
wades forth in galoshes
and a silver slicker
brandishing a steel rake.

This time of year you can leave
the door open.
The mosquitos haven't come out
though the cherry trees bloom and the red camellias
and the pure white pears.

This time of year it's good to swallow
black tea with honey and split the pink
shells of the salted hallucinatory pistachios,
watching the young mothers
in sweatshirts and jeans
who are just the right age to be porn stars
bundle their children into a green van
and drive away through the rain.

Courtly

No matter the high-flown improbable phrases,
the tinned fish and flowers, lipstick
and wine—no matter Venice's
gimcrack cornices
holding their arms apart in the night
or the red dahlias swaying on long stems
walloping each other in the summer wind.

It isn't the blue rocks at low tide
or the long grass by the sea wall,
lady of time and dried white flowers,
lady of distant rain

who wanders off looking for a book of matches
along the road near the coffee shop
built to look like a chateau
and spattered with bird shit
where gulls and ravens
like the Hollywood movies
have feasted for over a century
on the corpses of Lancelot and Keats.

Nobody knows what it's cost you
to keep facing up to the world like this
with its airport exhaust and chalk dust,
both of us tired, both of us cold,
trying to talk with the professors
and lonely for California.

I bring these today to the door
of your dream, as close
as I can approach:

saltwater to heal your sinuses,
coffee with soy milk and coconut,
blanket to warm your shoulders,
bag of blue ice for your spine.

Southern Exposure

Bring me your silent lake in the woods
and your field of harvested grain

with some rich man's horse pastured nearby,
its eyes pearlescent, its tangled mane.

Bring your late November rain,
your hurricane plywood and muscle car

the sounds of lovemaking under the bridge,
your troublesome blurry stars.

It's a winter Sunday in the pine-tar South
and the gray sky like distant satin

covers the roads and the smoky woods
where mash whiskey cooks in a kettle

and Lincoln's ghost squats in Oakwood Cemetery
bent down, counting the Confederate dead.

It's a scientific fact that it takes a year
for the earth to go around the sun

and I'm still a stranger in this world
of the battle lost and the battle won

though a pound of cotton weighs the same
as a pound of tendon or bone

and there might be a copperhead fast asleep
under the funeral home

for sometimes the blues moans like a prayer
and sometimes it spits out a curse

and even if you can't see all the scars
you can tell if something hurts.

Mothers

If you can walk
you should follow the shining canal
past the café's outdoor bar
hung with a gold canvas awning,
past the young men playing petanque,
rolling the silver balls on bare ground
near where they tie up the big riverboat
with its long red coach house
shaped like an egg and its rudder
shaped like a spoon.

If you can walk
you should follow the river
that winds its way south
like a vein,
for it's Mother's Day in America
and they are bringing the roses and lilacs,
the daisies and crook-necked star lilies,
pistils and stamens, petals and leaves.

They are working to make a pastry,
dusting their palms with cake flour and light—
it's shaped like a breast
like an unshed tear
like a ribbon that won't come untied.

Night Light

We've just managed to fall into bed
like the proprietors of a vacant hotel,
its garden smelling of quince and magnolia.
The pale moon spills in
like slivers of glass
through the dark cypress branches,
with the Oprah channel on low,
and the young father's husky voice
planning the next phase of his sex change.
His chestnut ringlets cover his collarbone,
framing his dark eyes
like a pale lady in Swinburne

and I'm trying to remember the day
that's ending, drifting away toward sleep:
I can feel my feet a long way down
where the world ends
and my body begins
and my hair would be fanned out
like smoke on the pillow, and my breasts
would be resting gently,
pendulous, mammalian
inside the haze of my nightgown.
I hear his voice a long way off:
they will somehow turn
his penis inward
to fashion a blind vagina
capable of deep sensation,
capable of loving a man.

Ronnie: 1954 – 2013

Ronnie's eyes are bloodshot and steady
under his iron-colored hair
and the wind keeps making mine
blink and tear
outside the noon Meeting
while he tells me about the 20-dollar
Tuesday Night Life-Drawing Class,
about quitting art school years ago
out west in California
to become a private detective,
the same year Nixon got re-elected
only to resign from office:
no more Bishoff and Diebenkorn,
no more mute wisdom of canvas and line,
no more Joan Brown and David Park,
his green skiff in the estuary,
picnic rain on the banks

and if the body is the world's last hotel,
its vestibules worn by time,
he will have checked out early
and be waiting outside alone
relaxing in one of those woven blue chairs,
in no big hurry to go anywhere
and admiring with his painter's eye
the earth's accidental beauty
which never can last—
the daylight moon overhead
as well as the splashes of last night's rain
which have settled the clouds of tree pollen
into pale green aqueous streaks
the color of ancient burnished metal
on the dark flat stones of the terrace.

Monk

Monk sat alone under the stars
dim and few as they were,
incognito on a park bench
with nothing to pawn
and nothing to fence,
his large fingers flexed
then halfway clenched.
He was thinking of music
the way a regular person
might be thinking of lunch.

He was thinking of Ruby
and thinking of tears,
some chords he could thumb left-handed,
some mathmatical renegade harmonics,
and maybe a tall cold gin and tonic,
not to mention a melody
that would sound like running downstairs.

He could think about music anywhere,
brushing his hair or tying his shoes.
Sometimes it sounded like ragtime or stride
or some geological landscape—
mineral and rock, volcanic shale,
lying just under the blues—
with its minor tones
muffled deep in the earth,
its phrasings that lasted
an extra beat,
which others could study
though no one could tell
what storms raged under his hat's

pinched crown
and over the quiet shores of his heart,
what polar tides rose
and fell down.

Bad Love Affair

You walk the night back
circling the park, pollen
stuck to your eyebrows and hair—
oak pollen, jasmine,
clouds of green rust
shedding onto your sleeves.

You are like a man in a film noir
whose plan for the week
is to keep moving and stay
out of sight. Each step you take
with your collar turned up
the night grows larger inside you,
stars, the sparks from a lit cigarette
thrown down onto Dolores Street,
glint of empty Corona bottles, wisps
of blond hair left behind on your pillow.

How long will you be so bereft?
Alone after hours in the dark cantina
watching clips of the great '80s middleweights:
Hagler and Leonard, Roberto Duran
or Tommy Hearns from Detroit
who would smile in the ring
like he had a secret
every time he was hurt.

Field

I sat down in the yellow chair
in the hush before the rain
watching the women walking together
through the glass door in their fulsome skin.
It was better than sleeping,
better than gin
with the immense heaven far overhead
the color of lead or beaten tin.

I saw their shirts loosely darkened
after the small drops began,
I saw their ribs and hips and hair
and it looked as though they were floating
across the electric air.

The election raged on in the cities
and death came in the night
for the famous judge—
whatever it is that resists transformation
must have abandoned him—
maybe the iron in the blood.

And then the rain opened its silver wings
beating down on the grasses
combed back by the wind
and the trees and plants
with their roots and seeds,
their blossoms and delicate limbs.

Language

Her fallen arch which you bend across
kissing the knobs of her feet, the patchy glaze

of her toenails rendering you half drunk
in the heat. Why not forget your mother's voice

scattered like ashes in the surf, the saltwater
trenches and ocean caverns' violent fiery birth.

Shot through with holes, the place you were born
buzzing with locusts, hornets and flies,

a gray dove nests below your window
listening to her mate's anonymous cry,

the estuary spread like an aging hand,
the paring-knife moon and two-lane bridge

and your lips which are grazing her ankle now
the tongue's flat muscle, the palate's ridge

echoing the doorway of childhood's
language, its trances of taste and smell,

the sounds formed somewhere back of the teeth
and shaped in the mouth's vestibule.

Community Hospital

for Susan

Here in the white kingdom
of padded metal and tiny lights
of oxygen gauges and hemoglobin

time trickles slowly down from above
and the most important thing
is the unbroken skin

on the nurse's forearm
reaching to hang the dark bag of blood.

Often at evening the light will settle
like honey on the bottom
of the bamboo curtain

where the long work of dying is carried on
through the birth pangs happening
two floors down

and she wants to be passive now
her eyes half closed, turning away
like Eurydice into the dark

past the hushed voices in the corridor
the faint smell of ether and gauze

the five lanes of rush hour
miles away in the wind,
like someone gently breaking away,
or the sound of the ocean's waves,
common and steady,
rising out of a shell.

The Poetry-Body

for K.D.

The youngest won't fall asleep
though he keeps resting his head on the table
next to his empty plate.
These are the jewels of his
half-open eyes bewitched by the pale
blossoming spines of the centerpiece flowers
no one remembers the names of—
these are the sparks flying up
from the fire and the night
pressing in on the windows.

I know by now the harsh stillness
of a winter night by the beach,
the moon half hidden
low and dim
and sometimes I think
poetry has failed me,
the nights gone by and chances missed
all breathing deeply beside me—
"a fluttering of feathers,"
you called it,
this soft body that consumes everything,
especially our failures
carrying something under its tongue
it is not going to show
to anyone.

"Yes, like a king halted in the great forest of Pennsylvania."

—Jack Gilbert

Persephone

Maybe she's traveled
from beyond the galaxy
past the sheets of blue light
and the gas filaments flaring
at the edge of the void
to sit by herself in our half-lit room
nursing a cold with Red Rose tea
and watching the small TV,
a mystery starring Robert Mitchum
wearing a Hawaiian shirt.
Everywhere the trash truck stops
she hears the hydraulics sing to themselves,
the white stars of spring
grown slowly dim

and probably she wants to go back,
maybe at least as far as Venus,
planet of love
with its opposite rotation
and single days
that last almost 6,000 hours.

But I know the storm front moving in
over the mountains from Tennessee,
I know the finches and dogwood branches,
the train yard's gravel and rusty spikes
have taken hold of her heart—
like the country market's tamales and aspirin,
its tangled dead kudzu and purple phlox,
like the vacant lot on the corner
broken open and gashed by rain.

Eclipse

Linden branches and narrow streets,
frost and ice on the full solstice moon

the first in 300 years this day
to suffer a total eclipse

though there's plenty of snow and daylight
yet to fall through the branches

each day lasting a minute longer
all the way up to spring.

Now you can make a wish
for the new year, now you

can lie awake in the dawn
listening to the plow's hydraulic blade

and the old dog that howls at the stars.
It can be hard to sleep in America

land of ceaseless wind and weather,
granite slabs and the sea breaking over them

traveling thousands of miles.
But you are the curious unfaltering one,

alive in the rouged earth-shadow
who combs out the knots in the dog's gray fur

and kisses the lover in the hidden mouth
and knows the moon will come back.

The Day After Sinatra Married Mia Farrow

So the coffee would stay hot all morning
Edna, the large-boned Dutch waitress,
her face and throat flushed from the heat
would first fill my thermos with boiling water
in the Circle Diner on Kutztown Road,
this July morning steamy and loud
with a highway crew at the counter,
two grizzled mailmen in the side booth
and us from the nearby construction site,
a job I loved for its noise and fresh air,
screwing big lag bolts into the sills
of Caloric Stove's new factory warehouse,
the whirr of the countersink drilling the wood,
clean white hemlock or spruce

and when one of the mailmen heads for the door
Edna calls out, *Hey Jack*
how you think Frank's feeling this morning?
Smoke from the grill and the cook's cigar
clouding the wide glass window:
Frank, 30 years her senior,
stepping from Sam Giancana's limo
or else whispering One for My Baby
into the spotlight: His death
in his voice with its flawless control,
his slanted fedora and raincoat,
his glittering life we could only imagine

though most of us are laughing by now
wolfing our hot cakes and eggs
when the old man yells back, *Tired as hell!*
pulling his hat down low at the door,

happy enough to be going to work
on a Friday under the dawnwashed sky
of Johnson's Great Society,
with the Lehigh Valley opening its thighs
and the weekend gorged with promise.

California

Sometimes the afternoon train
looks like pieces of fallen sky
chained together, liquid and slow
turning under the bluffs,
the gondola cars and the rumbling wheels,
big vein stretching in the brakeman's thigh
luminous under his black wool pants,
farther than dream, farther than thought
into the dusk of summer.

The following wind rustles the briars,
firstborn wind
blown down the track
over the market stalls
where the young mother walks,
her only child
looking out from her arms at the daylight
resting on lemons and corn.

No rain for weeks in the valley
for the ravens and crows
with their shank-beaks,
and the canyon wren
with its feet like hands,
no rain for weeks on the almond groves
blotting the morning dew.

Before we knew words for it
we loved the light
at rest on the sill
of the nursery window,
silver and gray on the vineyards,
pale blue-slate on the wheat.

Oxygen and Acetylene

As I stand in the door, talking on
about poetry and courtly love,
the unattainable woman
and the delicate Arabic forms,
he keeps looking past me
at the small bat that swoops
through the sawdusted air
and shits on the drill press
and band saw,
the welding tanks and the torch
he got at a bargain price back home
from a man going through a divorce.

Torch Singer

I could imagine her yellow skirt
rustling like a late summer breeze
over the mesh of her nylons
walking downstage, holding the mic
against her mouth
like a piece of intimate hardware
and sighing the lyrics to Cry Me a River.

That's how I thought of Julie London
before I heard she married Jack Webb,
Dragnet's favorite TV cop
who took such pride in being square
you could almost like him:
"Just tell us what happened, ma'am,
that's what we're here for."
Always faintly aloof and admonitory
in his narrow tie and brogan shoes,
always clean-shaven and matter of fact.
How could she marry a guy like that?

But the streets of LA and its nightclubs
were like some dazzling, forbidden realm
far from Western Pennsylvania
with its sandlot baseball and bloody nose,
its slag piles and abandoned mines.

I was trying to grow an imagination
from newsreels and cowboy movies,
not to mention the gorgeous shape
of the music teacher's ass
and the muscle cars like the Rocket 88,
somebody's uncle's pride and joy

with 18 layers of ivory baked
onto the fenders and deck lid,
and Gene Vincent in his pompadour
singing Woman Love from the dashboard.
And so I knew Julie was too good for him.
I watched the pale moths double in the air
and dreamed again of her husky voice,
her long legs and long auburn hair.

Night

Nobody wants to fall asleep
watching the stars burn like trash fires
listening to the big waves smoke
down the rocks,
nobody wants to sleep.

My Pelikan 800 fountain pen,
green with a faint gold stripe,
lost with my hundred-proof memory,
my sea flat as glass,
its kelp leaves and poppies.

Now I watch the women
dressed in black—black shoes,
black pants, long hair falling
over their hands and wrists.
They stay awake far into the night
writing their scattered poems,
sisters of the half-empty wine jar,
of childhood lost
in the coastal fog and the lapsed
Catholic funeral flowers.

Nobody thinks of going to sleep
now that the streetcars are silent,
now that the dew seeps
into the grass.
I came west in my twenties
looking for work,
driving straight into the setting sun
and now I'll take anything:
a pencil stub and a cheap
cardboard notebook
somebody gave me for nothing.

For Ruth Stone

Sometimes I say bad things about people
claiming it can't be helped

I crawl farther into the darkness
just to see what it feels like

but today I count the late frozen stars
and Jupiter drifting into the dawn

because Ruth the poet died last night
who listened to the muse alone:

the mailman and the trash truck driver
the women who work in Lost and Found

faded hair wispy as cotton gauze
in the discount store downtown.

One is folding a dark wool sweater
that smells of camphor and lighter fluid

in one worn pocket a bus ticket
from Roanoke to Syracuse.

The creaky hinge on the Ladies Room door
silent now in the vacant station

only a traveling woman asleep
her suitcase tied with ribbons and twine

and snowflakes dusting the platform
their stellar dendrites and crystal rosettes

flickering like signals from outer space
planetary and blind.

Girlfriends

They come jittering into her life from the past,
brunette like her mother, wiry
and tense, wearing garments black
as anthracite chopped from the city's heart.
Complaint rises like music or smoke
past the elegant lamps of their faces
as they settle their fringe and nail polish
onto our secondhand couch: men, mostly,
but the theme could be anything,
children, money, uterine cramping,
low brilliant choruses of damage and pain.

They tell her their dreams, of roses
and falling. They point to the crow's feet
deepening each year above
the wings of their cheekbones.

In the one painting my mother left
when she died, the waves are breaking
over Folly Cove. All night they will break
in the autumn dark, while one friend sleeps
holding onto her boy-lover and another
drives south through the rain-soaked hills
bound for her sister's third wedding. They
carry the yoke of the city's blue lights
easily back toward morning. They feel
their bodies grow beautiful, the night sky
smoothing their faces and hair. Nobody
needs to tell them death's hands
keep opening over the road.

Artist Colony

You'd like to be home
watching re-runs of Kojak
busting crooks in the big city canyons
cruising an unmarked V-8 Lincoln,
his stingy-brim slantwise on his shaved scalp—
a .45 in his coat—
pulling a lollipop
from his thick lips
and saying, "Who loves ya, baby?"

It's fun to think of him,
now deceased, enjoying
an easy old age from residuals,
maybe some golf,
a little backgammon,
more likely a day at the track
where he once owned a thoroughbred
named Telly's Pop
that won the Del Mar Futurity
though you lost 40 bucks
when you bet him to win
the same year at Bay Meadows.

And now you sit quietly
in the large common room
listening to the music of two composers
younger than most of your children:
music of glass and magnetized metal,
music of searchlights in outer space.

Outside, the finches keep eating seeds
from the spiked orange crowns

of the candle flowers
and the black horse in the pasture
you fed all those apples and carrots
no longer seems to remember you.

Why Women Live Longer

You can hear two thin minor chords
through the wall and the song
in a broken falsetto
as you lie on the couch
half out of your body
unable to feel your feet—
dead leaves blowing off the tin roof
just ahead of the rain—
then something about a coal mine,
something about a train.

You don't like her to see you like this
though she knows you well,
your socks fallen down and the rough hair
all worn away from your shins
which are shiny now
like an old man's
which is what you're becoming
this afternoon, listening to faint music,
watching the shadows drift
down the gray ceiling, stained
like a liver X-ray.

She comes in the house with her girlfriend,
they soldier along through the desert of time.
They rub lotion into their aging calves
speaking of shoes, speaking of hair,
the tea roses climbing the mailbox.
If you could you would visit
your father's ashes, long since
scattered on Lighthouse Beach,
no matter the feeling of rootlessness,
of night coming on and the early stars
almost out of reach.

Penn Station

The sky is a confusion of scars
lightning bolts and black clouds
piled up over Madison Garden
where Sugar Ray Robinson beat Jake La Motta
and Henry Armstrong and everyone else,
and where you're waiting downstairs
for the 91 Silver Star to Miami
currently suffering engine problems.
No one knows when we leave.

No one knows the grooved iron rails
like these old conductors and brakemen,
no one knows the trouble they've seen,
the Time Zones of cinders and gravel dust,
the crossties and metal flanges
pocked and stippled with rust.

You're hoping to get home by nightfall
chomping a Nathan's with fries
and trying to finish your postmodern novel
packed with footnotes and ironic digressions,
narcissism and suicide,
and they call out the train to Pittsburgh,
the train to New Brunswick, NJ

that rumbles over the tracks below
out of the tunnel and onto the plains
of sedge grass and swampland, ashes and trash
billowing up below the embankment
and the neighbors watching from their backyards,
home from work in their dusty shoes,
their asphalt shingles and chimney flues
rocking under the jittering stars.

Valentine

It's February in North Carolina,
the day before Valentine's Day,
and we listen to the elegant waves
quiet and monstrous, grinding away

at the sand's fractured layers
of feldspar and quartz, the dunes'
dark gray cactus and pampas grass,

the incoming tide we walk beside
drinking take-out coffee
stooping down every now and then
to pick up a shell or a smooth piece of glass

and talking about an old friend
now sailing a southern ocean
who doesn't want to come back to land

more afraid of contentment
and the slow trance of age
than the elements of the deep,
maybe thinking it would be no great outrage
to die on the water, like falling asleep—

tired like the rest of us
and not willing to admit it:
even the wars of baseball
even love's politics
even the slab-sided salmon
hauled up for years on his decks—

and maybe dreaming like Coleridge
of rocking forever in the blue void
like a floating abandoned wreck.

I make us turn back when we reach the pier
weary of walking, wanting to lie down,
our footprints already disappearing
under the shrouds of foam.

One of the things I like about you
is the way you can leave things alone

with your hat pulled low over your hair
and your face partly hidden below,
stepping pigeon-toed next to me
watching the distant whitecaps flare

and the strong wings of sea birds
relentless and young
beating high up in the air.

Patience

How long must we wait, composer,
for the slender moon
to shine down its light
on piano keys turned yellow with age,
for the living, ordinary notes
of the nocturne
to divide the crimes of pretending
from the crime of falling asleep?

I'm afraid of the oil
rising into the Gulf
where the drilling rig has exploded,
the black snake climbing the fence post
to swallow the catbird's eggs.

How long till the fat man lying back
in the next room
holding the guitar to his chest
like a piece of wreckage
keeping him afloat
opens his mouth to sing?

You reach out your hand
like the messiah of pawn shops,
of late-night trains
coming down from the north,
the flute in its dark red velvet case
beginning to tarnish and fade. . . .

You reach out your other hand
over the brick work,
wide awake in the dazzle of spring,
coal dust fallen like pollen
on the window glass and the shade.

Roses

for S.G.

If you don't show up today
you will miss the fountain
shedding its torn shroud
over and over,
the baby asleep
in her yellow dress
and the flame-shaped conifers
near the entrance
smelling of last night's rain.

It's early Easter and no one
has seen him
since they rolled back the stone,
not even the Magdalene.
Is he in heaven, is he in hell
hiding among the roses?
The red ones that cover the arbor
or the ones dyed blue
that arrived in the night
sent by some secret admirer
whose name the florist
promised not to reveal?

Maybe he's watched you leave home
each day, carrying your shoes in a bag:
the red ones for running,
the brown ones for work.
Maybe he follows you to the bus stop,
then walks through the Natural History Museum
gazing up at the blue-whale skeleton,
its jaws and ribcage,
trying to imagine the size of its heart,
then sits in the dollar movies alone
like a lover who can't forget you.

Making Lunch

Because nothing I see this morning
brings us closer to spring,
snow falling out of the Jersey sky
into the cloudy river,
wet shoes facing toe-in,
uppers spotted with rock salt

and because each sound signifies winter—
wind in the wires and the far-off train
like the voice of a child
circling the planet
looking for a place to be born—

I spread out the mustard
like a gold map
over the slabs of rye
and lay down the sliced mozzarella
holding the tomatoes for last

because they are acid and red
and grow on a clustered vine
staked up in a cage
in another country
of sunlight and olives

where children run barefoot
chasing a rusty bicycle rim
and the grass clumps up
through cracks in the bricks
next to a stone bridge scaled
with gray lichen, and the warm earth
swollen with black truffle fungi,
smells of bay leaves and wine.

Lovesick

Why don't you just say one of your prayers,
she sighs on the way to the airport

passing through the Virginia hills,
something hidden and dazed in her look

like Dylan's corrosive voice
smoldering out of the radio.

When we stop to stretch
in a grove of dark pines

she looks like she's trying
to remember something

standing beside the fender
and bending the wing mirror over:

I look okay in this gray light, she says
no one can see my crow's feet.

I can't decide if she's flirting with me
or trying to pick a fight.

What if I tell her I'm not afraid
of her riddles and midnight rages?

What if I hand her these scrawny violets
and just say, Get back in the car?

Ancestral

Sometimes the bent ghost of my father
holding a dead Pall Mall in its teeth
walks the sandy track to the beach
he called "my garden"
where he would lie on his stomach reading:
a book about astronomy
or the history of music,
maybe a seed catalog.
The channel a deep blue
passing the lighthouse,
split slabs of granite
heaped up on the shore,
saltwater sparkling in the cuts.

I like it when the flood tide
surges in once a month
overcoming the land,
seawater rising under the face
of the pale stone
gazing down from the heavens,
veiling her dark side
where some people claim
entire cities exist.

I like to write with this space pen
given to me by a friend,
the same one the astronauts use.
I fall asleep with the milky way
wrapped around my shoulders.
I like the burned methane clouds
and the black threads of iron
sunk deep in the stars, and the earth
where it's sometimes cast into bells—

bells of evening, bells of death,
bells of some ruthless joy—
iron that floats like salt in the bloodstream,
plasma inheritance, proteins and enzymes,
two million red cells every second
born in the body's jubilant fire,
the deep cells of the marrow.

Reckoning

I would pay double
to escape these ledgers
forced upon me by my accountant,
he of the cat smile and fine moustache
and the huge conference room
with blue walls
like the sea off of Costa Rica
or maybe the Cayman Islands.

Señor, I would like to say,
look at this flood of receipts
rising in the gray March air:
these were the new front tires for the car
these were the stamps
and the cell phone bills,
these were 500 café lattes
which I swilled
through a plastic orifice
sitting alone in the front seat
waiting for my wife to get off work.

Señor, this year I stole nothing of value:
a fisheye lens for my wing mirror
which then broke off in the car wash,
a green avocado,
a ballpoint pen
but I know I've claimed too many miles,
too many restaurant dinners.

I went to the movies and saved the stub
which I know I can never write off,
and then I came home

and slept in my bed
dreaming of prison like Al Capone
suffering with syphilis on Alcatraz,
instead of Karl Marx and Noam Chomsky,
Joe Hill or Eugene Debs,
instead of the hammer and sickle,
the starry plough and raised fist.

Black Pan

Let the evening spread over the garden
like the broad skirts of a mother
covering the windy potato plants
with their pale blossoms fluttering,
the spuds on their stems
having grown up from their parents' eyes
clothed in a delicate skin,
then slow-cooked with oil in a black pan,
eaten with salt and white chicken meat
on the night of the equinox.

I stole this round point shovel from work
with its fine-grained handle
and shiny blade
right after I twisted my back
the last day pouring some concrete stairs
on a job where there wasn't much shade.

And now the sun shines down just the same
over the equator
so the night will last as long as the day
and Orion will appear with his belt and sword
before dawn, over the front porch
where my wife sits with her iPhone
picking up messages from outer space.
I can hear the straw chair
rock back and forth
I hear her deep sigh at summer's end.

Will we have music? Will we have rain?
Listening to autumn coming down close
with its rake and scythe,

stepping gently between the rows
over the mulch and fallen leaves
the celery, garlic, beets and chives
unmindful of injury or pain.

Calling Home

for E.C.

Language has always come to you broken
sporadic and hard to breathe,
its night air black
as a typewriter ribbon
imprinted with autumn stars,
its movie tickets and fast food wrappers,
lipstick and postage stamps.
At your back the vast Carolina woods
their red leaves and kudzu,
wind from the south,
blown sparks of phosphorus
like the breath of a traveling saint—
saint of the money order
wired on the first,
saint of the Sunday phone call.

No one's out on the road today,
nobody in the fields.
You stop to call on the bridge
over the Cape Fear river,
nobody on the river.
When a tree falls this far from home
who shall say there's no sound,
its limbs breaking off in the silence,
its roots prized up from the earth?
And the signal keeps traveling west-southwest
thousands of miles to the desert,
money for a nephew's school books,
money for jeans and a soccer jersey,
the staccato phrases' filial music
wide awake on your tongue.

Clair de Lune

We started back from the coast
in the darkness, the long bus
watching out for black ice
with evergreen branches on either side,
sea wind pushing us
up from the beach
and five or six people coughing,
everyone trying to rest . . .

on a morning like this
the sky draws close,
you can see the faint stars,
a strand of blue fog half covering
the fulsome, promiscuous moon.
Everyone knows
she'll go home with anybody,
even you in your secondhand shirt
with aspirin in the front pocket,

your tongue asleep
in your mouth like a reef fish
tasting of smoke and wine,
its songs left behind on the ribbed sand
abandoned there by the ebb:
song of watching the crab boats at night,
song of watering the houseplants.

She'll follow you home
to your skeletal orchard, your barn
with its wisps of hay,
though she surely won't let you sleep,
hours from sunrise over the driveway
shining into your kitchen.

They say she went home
with Stanley Kubrick in 1968,
posed naked under his arc lights,
lay on her back while the astronauts
gathered their fragments of feldspar,
planted their spindly flags.

She shines on the bus driver's
blond ponytail,
she's making big eyes at him,
his hands on the wheel
with their black leather cuffs,
shines on the sheet metal
covering the engine
and the road's thin shoulder
speckled with rock salt
hunched against the dawn.

Dandelion

"Each flower head is composed of thousands
of small ray-flowers."
—Oregon State University Department of Horticulture

Someone's neglected the dandelion
with its flower that looks like a face,
its dim seed-globe and its nasty wine,
its toothed green leaves and its twisted root
you can brew into an inglorious tea
which will soothe the kidneys
and purify the liver
and may even cure hepatitis C

brought on no doubt
by a misspent youth
lying around without a job
not eating enough root vegetables
high in minerals and vitamin B,
shooting dope with a dirty needle
and watching too much TV.

It grows in the lawn and the outfield
and doesn't need to cross-pollinate
the way you've carried on with multiple partners
in run-down motels and ragged back seats.
The dandelion is no flash in the pan,
no one-night stand
that wilts in the dawn.
It opens its face to the midday sun
but it's not trying to get a tan.

Paris Rain

for the roofers

You can hear them sing on the scaffold
dragging their metal ladders across,
you can hear the rough steel bang
like fine brass
just below your windows
where the heavy bell of the little church
hangs from its cast iron crown
and the roofers gather together
smoking Gauloise in the rain.

Nobody wants to be really alone
eating a lunch of stone bread
and salami, unless it's the foreman
parked down the block
hiding beneath his woolen hat
cocked low over the noonday calm

and nobody wants to wake in the dark
among leafy gargoyles and mansard roofs,
misremembering how they arrived,
their work forgotten, their tools and boots,
their gravity left behind in the air
like a bee who can't find the hive.

You listen to the sound of the Paris rain
the bells of the church
and the ladder's clang
your jet-lag dreams of Xanax and wine,
of escape from the narrow fields of time
of no one to ask and no one to blame
one and the same
in the hands of the rain.

End of the World

December 21, 2012

Everyone's still waking up this day
listening to the Angelus bells
or maybe listening to neighborhood gunfire:
here at the end of the Mayan calendar
with its cycles of Venus
and Lords of the Night

the cold wind
gusting out of the north
so the wren puffs its feathers

and the lights on the blue spruce,
splinters of ice
flicker and burn by the window.

Season of holly berries and dead leaves,
darkness and distant stars,

the sweet time taken
to build a fire

each stroke of the broom
sweeping the hearth
each sheet of newsprint
with its gambler's heart:

the day's price of gold,
its lies and wars
crumpled into a ball,

each stick laid in and tilted up,
ingots of white pine, maple and oak

and the smell of burnt sap
rising into the smoke. . . .

Everyone's still waking up
in their beds or a ditch

or the one metal bench
under the airport's cold steel roof
looking up at the lights of the Milky Way
which the Mayans called the Crocodile Tree . . .

and I fall in love in the morning
thousands of miles below

watching your feet through the doorway
walking out into the first day of winter

with its broken sunlight
and haphazard weather,
its frozen mud and new snow

its blackened roses and jaguar tears
falling for 5,000 years.

Notes

"The Poem of Experience" is for David St. John.
"Right Livelihood" is for Dorianne Laux.
"Time-Poem" is for David Garratt.
"Muse" is for Alex Reams.
"Next to Godliness" is for Jay Nebel.
"Night Light" is for Marie Howe.
"Southern Exposure" is for Wilton Barnhardt.
"Ronnie" is for Ron Long.
"Bad Love Affair" is for Tim McBride.
"Community Hospital" is for Susan Adams.
"The Poetry-Body" is for Kwame Dawes.
"Oxygen and Acetylene" is for Steve Torre.
"Roses" is for Sierra Golden.
"Making Lunch" is for Nancy Hechinger.
"Ancestral" is for Michael McGriff.
"Calling Home" is for Eduardo Corral.

Photo: Michael Selker

Joseph Millar is the author of three previous collections. His poems have won fellowships from the Guggenheim Foundation and the NEA. He teaches in Pacific University's Low Residency MFA and divides his time between Raleigh, North Carolina, and Richmond, California.